D1195255

OCEANS ALIVE

Manta Rays

by Colleen Sexton

BELLWETHER MEDIA • MINNEAPOLIS, MN

Note to Librarians, Teachers, and Parents:

Blastoff! Readers are carefully developed by literacy experts and combine standards-based content with developmentally appropriate text.

Level 1 provides the most support through repetition of high-frequency words, light text, predictable sentence patterns, and strong visual support.

Level 2 offers early readers a bit more challenge through varied simple sentences, increased text load, and less repetition of high-frequency words.

Level 3 advances early-fluent readers toward fluency through increased text and concept load, less reliance on visuals, longer sentences, and more literary language.

Level 4 builds reading stamina by providing more text per page, increased use of punctuation, greater variation in sentence patterns, and increasingly challenging vocabulary.

Level 5 encourages children to move from "learning to read" to "reading to learn" by providing even more text, varied writing styles, and less familiar topics.

Whichever book is right for your reader, Blastoff! Readers are the perfect books to build confidence and encourage a love of reading that will last a lifetime!

This edition first published in 2010 by Bellwether Media, Inc.

Library of Congress Cataloging-in-Publication Data
Sexton, Colleen A., 1967-
Manta Rays / by Colleen Sexton.
p. cm. – (Blastoff! readers. Oceans alive)
Includes bibliographical references and index.
Summary: "Simple text and full color photographs introduce beginning readers to manta rays. Developed by literacy experts for students in kindergarten through third grade"–Provided by publisher.
ISBN 978-1-60014-267-3 (hardcover : alk. paper)
1. Mobulidae–Juvenile literature. I. Title.

QL638.85.M6S48 2009
597.35–dc22

2009008479

Contents

Manta rays are fish. They live in warm ocean waters near land.

Manta rays can grow up to 22 feet (7 meters) wide.

A manta ray has a flat body.

Most manta rays are black, gray, or brown on top. Their undersides are white.

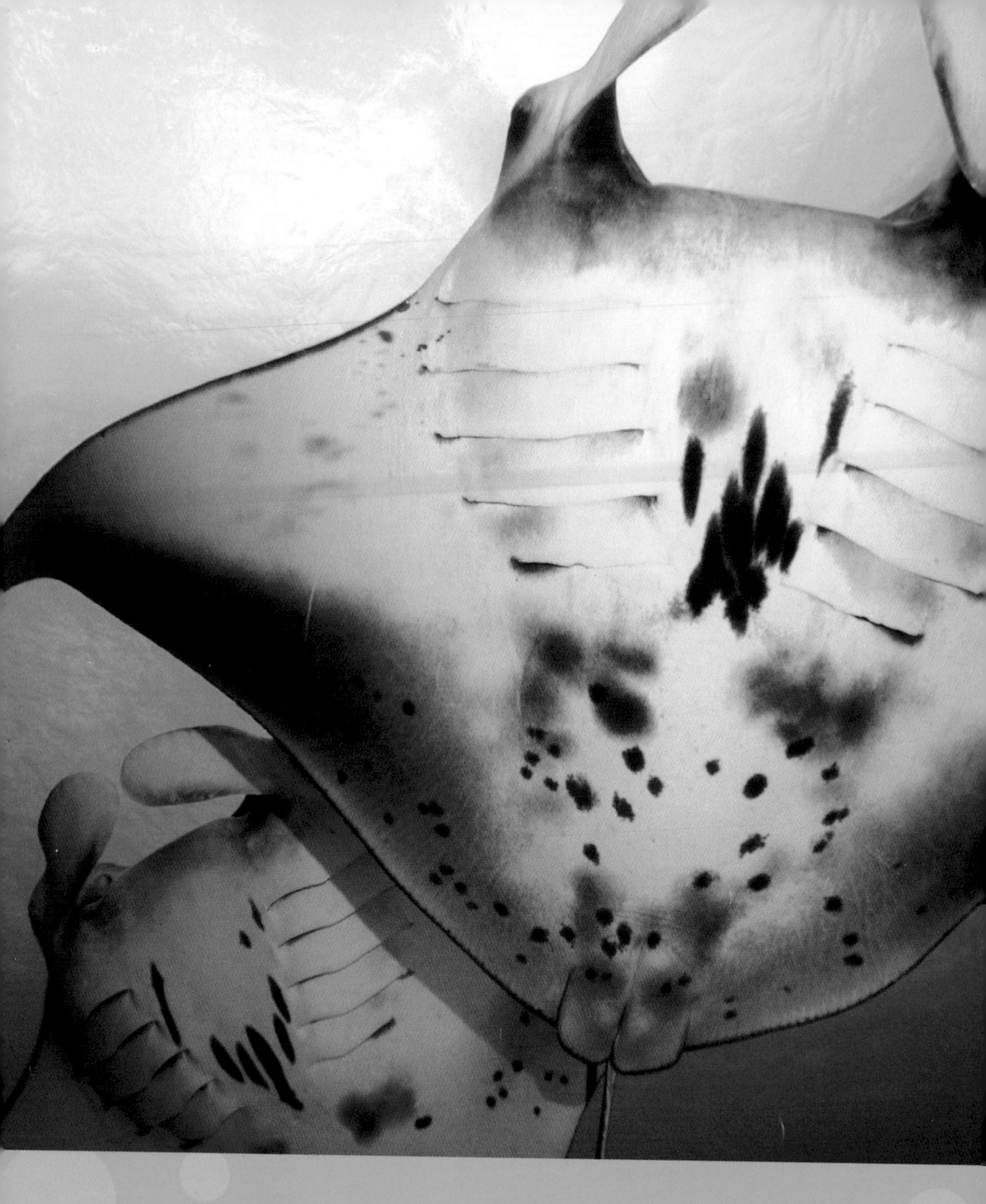

Some manta rays have light or dark patches. The patches make **patterns** on their skin.

Manta rays breathe through **gills**. Their gill slits are on their undersides.

Manta rays do not have bones. Their skeletons are made of **cartilage**.

Cartilage is light and rubbery.
It helps manta rays bend.

A manta ray has a thin tail that looks like a whip.

A manta ray has large **fins** that look like wings. They flap their fins up and down to swim.

A manta ray also has two small fins on either side of its head.

Manta rays roll up their small fins to swim fast. They unroll the fins when it is time to feed.

Manta rays use the fins to sweep **plankton** and small fish into their mouths.

A manta ray has a wide mouth.
Filters in the mouth catch food.

Manta rays let small fish eat the food left on their mouths. The fish clean their bodies, too.

The **cleaner fish** help manta rays stay healthy.

Manta rays can jump out of the water.

They soar through the air and
land with a splash!

Glossary

cartilage—a strong, bendable material; a manta ray's skeleton is made of cartilage.

cleaner fish—fish that clean larger ocean animals

filter—a hard part in a manta ray's mouth that lets water pass through but catches small fish and other ocean life

fins—the parts of an ocean animal used to move, steer, and stop in the water

gills—organs on a fish's body that it uses to breathe; gills move oxygen from the water to the fish's blood.

pattern—an arrangement of lines and shapes

plankton—tiny plants and animals that float in the ocean and are food for other animals

To Learn More

AT THE LIBRARY

Sill, Cathryn. *About Fish: A Guide for Children.* Atlanta, Ga.: Peachtree, 2002.

Sjonger, Rebecca, and Bobbie Kalman. *Skates and Rays.* New York, N.Y.: Crabtree, 2006.

Walker, Sally M. *Rays.* Minneapolis, Minn.: Carolrhoda Books, 2003.

ON THE WEB

Learning more about manta rays is as easy as 1, 2, 3.

1. Go to www.factsurfer.com.
2. Enter "manta rays" into the search box.
3. Click the "Surf" button and you will see a list of related Web sites.

With factsurfer.com, finding more information is just a click away.

The images in this book are reproduced through the courtesy of: Tomas Kotouc, front cover, p. 15; David Fleetham / Getty Images, p. 4; Stephen Frink / Getty Images, pp. 5, 9; Wolfgang Pölzer / Alamy, p. 6; Mike Veitch / Alamy, pp. 7, 8, 12-13, 16; James D. Watt / imagequestmarine.com, pp. 10-11; Brian Skerry / Getty Images, p. 14; Juniors Bildarchiv / age fotostock, p, 17; Hbbolten, pp. 18-19; Pat Bonish, p. 20; blickwinkel / Alamy, p. 21.